AUG 2 0 2019

W9-BHA-560

**St. Charles
Public Library**
St. Charles, IL 60174

COLIN
KAEPERNICK

COLIN
KAEPERNICK

FROM **FREE AGENT** TO **CHANGE AGENT**

Eric Braun

LERNER PUBLICATIONS ◆ MINNEAPOLIS

Copyright © 2020 by Lerner Publishing Group, Inc.

All rights reserved. International copyright secured. No part of this book may be reproduced, stored in a retrieval system, or transmitted in any form or by any means—electronic, mechanical, photocopying, recording, or otherwise—without the prior written permission of Lerner Publishing Group, Inc., except for the inclusion of brief quotations in an acknowledged review.

Lerner Publications Company
An imprint of Lerner Publishing Group, Inc.
241 First Avenue North
Minneapolis, MN 55401 USA

For reading levels and more information, look up this title at www.lernerbooks.com.

Image credits: Slaven Vlasic/Getty Images, p. 2; Michael Zagaris/Getty Images, pp. 6, 25, 29; JOY POWELL/AFP/Getty Images, p. 8; Thearon W. Henderson/Getty Images, pp. 9, 16; Harry How/Getty Images, p. 10; Debbie Noda/Modesto Bee/ZUMAPRESS./Newscom, p. 12; Bart Ah You/ZUMA Press/Newscom, p. 13; Steve Conner/Icon Sports Wire/Getty Images, p. 14; AP Photo/Steven Senne, p. 17; Focus on Sport/Getty Images, p. 18; Tim Clayton/Corbis Sport/ Getty Images, p. 19; Mark Wallheiser/Getty Images, p. 21; AP Photo/M. Spencer Green, p. 22; Stephen Maturen/Getty Images, p. 23; Jake Roth/USA Today Sports/Newscom, p. 24; Joe Amon/ The Denver Post/Getty Images, p. 26; Kevin C. Cox/Getty Images, p. 27; Marty Bicek/ZUMA Press, Inc./Alamy Stock Photo, p. 28; Brian Rothmuller/Icon Sportswire/Getty Images, p. 30; San Gabriel Valley Tribune/ ZUMA Press, Inc./Alamy Stock Photo, p. 31; HIROKO MASUIKE/The New York Times/Redux, p. 32; ANDREW CABALLERO-REYNOLDS/AFP/Getty Images, p. 33; AP Photo/Pablo Martinez Monsivais, p. 34; Andy King/Getty Images, p. 35; Nancy Lane/MediaNews Group/Boston Herald/Getty Images, p. 36; Robert O'neil/SplashNews/Newscom, p. 38; Robert Alexander/Archive Photos/Getty Images, p. 39; Matt Winkelmeyer/Getty Images, p. 40; AP Photo/Peter Dejong, p. 41.

Cover: Michael Zagaris/Getty Images.

Main body text set in Rotis Serif Std 55 Regular. Typeface provided by Adobe Systems.

Library of Congress Cataloging-in-Publication Data

Names: Braun, Eric.
Title: Colin Kaepernick : from free agent to change agent / Eric Braun.
Description: Minneapolis : Lerner Publications, [2020] | Series: Gateway biographies | Includes bibliographical references and index.
Identifiers: LCCN 2019012418 (print) | LCCN 2019014629 (ebook) | ISBN 9781541556195 (eb pdf) | ISBN 9781541556171 (lb : alk. paper) | ISBN 9781541574311 (pb : alk. paper)
Subjects: LCSH: Kaepernick, Colin, 1987– —Juvenile literature. | Football players—United States—Biography—Juvenile literature. | Football players—United States—Conduct of life.
Classification: LCC GV939.K25 (ebook) | LCC GV939.K25 B65 2020 (print) | DDC 796.332092 [B]—dc23

LC record available at https://lccn.loc.gov/2019012418

Manufactured in the United States of America
1-46073-43489-4/30/2019

CONTENTS

Colin Kaepernick and teammates kneel before the start of a game in 2016 as the national anthem plays in the stadium.

The first time he did it, nobody noticed. While his teammates stood for "The Star Spangled Banner," San Francisco 49ers quarterback Colin Kaepernick sat on the bench.

Why would anyone notice? It was a preseason game. Even in the National Football League (NFL), the most popular sports league in the United States, fans mostly ignore preseason games. The press covers them, and analysts discuss the highlights. But the games don't count in the season's standings, and the stars barely play. The preseason is just a warm-up.

Fans and players stand for the national anthem before NFL games, even in the preseason. And when the music started that day in August 2016, moments before the 49ers were to begin play, Colin Kaepernick made the most important decision of his life. He sat down.

Maybe a few people did notice him sitting. Some of his teammates, perhaps, or a reporter or two. But they would have assumed it didn't mean anything. It could have been a meaningless mistake. Kaepernick wasn't even in uniform

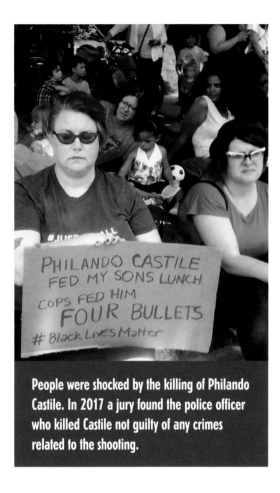

People were shocked by the killing of Philando Castile. In 2017 a jury found the police officer who killed Castile not guilty of any crimes related to the shooting.

that day—he had a sore shoulder and the team wanted him to rest.

But to Kaepernick, sitting during the national anthem was anything but a meaningless gesture. He sat to protest the mistreatment of black people and other people of color in the United States. Though this oppression was nothing new, recent events had upset Kaepernick.

News of police officers killing people of color had become more common in the past few years. Just a month before the game, a police officer near Minneapolis shot a black man named Philando Castile. He told the officer that he had a gun and a legal permit to carry it. Though Castile's girlfriend, who was in the car with him, said he did not reach for the gun, the officer shot him seven times. Castile's girlfriend livestreamed the tragedy on Facebook as Castile died next to her. The nation was shocked. Many assumed that the officer panicked because Castile was black. A few weeks later, this violent episode was still on the minds of Americans, including Kaepernick.

At the same time, the harsh, bruising campaign for US president was heating up. Some people believed candidate Donald Trump's speeches often had racist overtones. He stoked fears of immigrants and minorities. Some of his supporters were white nationalists, people who were openly racist and believed that nonwhites were inferior. Many Americans were alarmed.

Kaepernick's football career was at its peak when he became more involved with issues of social justice.

It was clear to Kaepernick that a century and a half after the abolition of slavery in the United States, racial injustice was still common. Racist beliefs were deeply embedded in many people who controlled US institutions such as the justice system. The more he thought about it, he realized he could not stand to honor the national anthem or the US flag. Not when they represented a country that ruthlessly oppressed some of its people.

Kaepernick sat again during the national anthem at the second preseason game. If anyone noticed, no one said anything publicly. So far, it was a silent protest.

The third preseason game of the year was August 26, 2016, against the Green Bay Packers. This time, Kaepernick was suited up. He was going to play. As with the first two preseason games, he sat on the bench during the national anthem. But unlike those protests, this time someone noticed. A reporter from NFL Media asked him after the game why he hadn't stood for the national anthem.

Kaepernick was ready for the question. "I am not going to stand up to show pride in a flag for a country that oppresses black people and people of color," he said. "To me, this is bigger than football and it would be selfish on my part to look the other way."

Another reporter asked if Kaepernick felt oppressed. He said that sometimes he felt poorly treated, but he wasn't protesting for himself. He was doing it to give a voice to people who didn't have one. Kaepernick had a platform—a job that let him capture the public's attention. Because he was a famous quarterback, people would listen to him about police brutality against

Kaepernick talked openly about his protest when asked by reporters.

people of color when they might not pay attention to others.

Many things were about to change for Kaepernick, though not all in the ways he hoped. The US flag and the national anthem are very important symbols to many people. To them, refusing to stand for the anthem was deeply disrespectful. They hated Kaepernick for it. He said he loved his country and wanted to make it better, but not everyone believed him. His silent protest was about to get very loud. It was about to turn his life upside down.

A Childhood in Sports

Colin was born on November 3, 1987, and adopted five weeks later. His birth mother, who was 19, wanted him to have a better life than she could provide at the time. She was white, and Colin's father was black. The couple that adopted him, Rick and Teresa Kaepernick, were white.

The Kaepernicks had two other children, and they wanted another baby. When the chance came to adopt Colin, they jumped at it. Teresa Kaepernick thought he was perfect.

Four years later, the Kaepernicks moved from Wisconsin to Turlock, California. The majority of people in Turlock were white, and only 2 percent of its residents identify as African American. When Colin was growing up, people often stared or gave his family funny looks. Sometimes

Colin with his parents, Teresa and Rick

strangers came up to him while he was standing with his family and asked if he was lost. They didn't believe Rick and Teresa Kaepernick and their two white children were Colin's family.

The Kaepernicks always made sure Colin felt that it was totally fine to have a different skin color from them. They let him express himself and explore his identity. "I never felt that I was supposed to be white," Colin said. "Or black, either. My parents just wanted to let me be who I needed to be."

As a high school student, Colin loved sports, and he was very good at football. He played quarterback and had a powerful arm. He also played basketball, but his best sport may have been baseball. He had a 94-mile-an-hour (151 km) fastball and started getting scholarship offers to play baseball in college. Colin dreamed of playing college football, but schools weren't offering him a football scholarship.

It looked as if Colin would never get an offer to play college football. Then one night an assistant football coach from the University of Nevada came to Colin's high school. Nevada coaches had watched tape of Colin, but they hadn't seen him play in person. Then it was

December, and football season was over. So the Nevada assistant, Barry Sacks, went to a basketball game. Colin had a fever of 102°F (39°C), but he still dominated the game. Sacks was blown away by Colin's athleticism and leadership. Sacks called the head coach at Nevada, Chris Ault, and told him he had found their next quarterback.

In high school, Colin could throw the ball as fast as many pro baseball players.

Nevada became the only school to offer Colin a football scholarship. It was a huge gamble for them—they had never even seen him play the sport in person. But they needed a quarterback, and they believed in Colin. He moved to Reno to join the University of Nevada Wolfpack.

As the team's backup quarterback, Kaepernick didn't play much at first as a freshman in 2006. His main task was to work out more and gain weight. He was tall and thin, and Wolfpack coaches worried he would be injured during games if he didn't add muscle. Kaepernick bulked up to 225 pounds (102 kg). In a game midway through the season, he racked up 420 combined passing and rushing yards with five touchdowns. He was the team's starter for the next three and a half years.

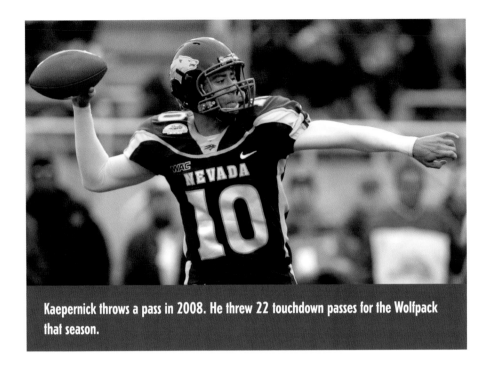

Kaepernick throws a pass in 2008. He threw 22 touchdown passes for the Wolfpack that season.

He still had a strong arm, and he was fast. Running became a key part of his game. His bigger size made him harder to tackle and less likely to be injured. As a threat to pass or run, he gave defenses headaches. In 2010, his final season, Nevada went 13–1. They beat third-ranked Boise State in overtime and finished the season ranked as the 11th-best team in the country. Before Kaepernick's arrival, Nevada had never made the national rankings at all. By the time he graduated, he had become the first player at college football's top level to throw for more than 10,000 yards and rush for more than 4,000.

Besides being an excellent college quarterback, Colin was a first-rate student and became involved in community service. He was curious about people's experiences. As he began to think more about race and identity, he explored African American culture and history. He joined a mostly black fraternity at Nevada, Kappa Alpha Psi, so he could explore a deeper connection to his own roots.

"Finding an identity was big for him," a college teammate said. "Because in some aspects in life, he would get the racist treatment from white people because he was a black quarterback. And some people gave him the racist treatment because he was raised by a white family. So where does he fit in?"

Where Colin Kaepernick fit in would become clear in a few years. But first, he declared himself eligible for the 2011 NFL Draft.

Super Bowl Quarterback

While it had been hard to get scouts to pay attention to Kaepernick in high school, it was a different story in college. He drew the interest of several NFL teams, and the 49ers chose him with their second-round draft pick.

Kaepernick was the backup to starting quarterback Alex Smith in 2011 and rarely played. San Francisco went 13–3, winning the division. The 49ers were defeated in the conference title game by the New York Giants, who went on to win the Super Bowl.

Smith remained the starter in 2012, but Kaepernick played in more games than the year before. He scored his first professional touchdown on a seven-yard run in the fourth game. Midway through the season, Smith suffered a concussion. Kaepernick replaced him in the game and completed 11 of 17 passes for 117 yards. For the first time, the NFL saw how his running ability could change a game, as he added 66 rushing yards and a rushing touchdown. The 49ers and St. Louis Rams tied 24–24.

Kaepernick started the next game against the Chicago Bears. He completed 16 of 23 passes for 243 yards with two touchdowns, and the 49ers won 32–7. Smith was a terrific quarterback with a 19–5–1 record. But when he was healthy enough to return, the team decided to stick

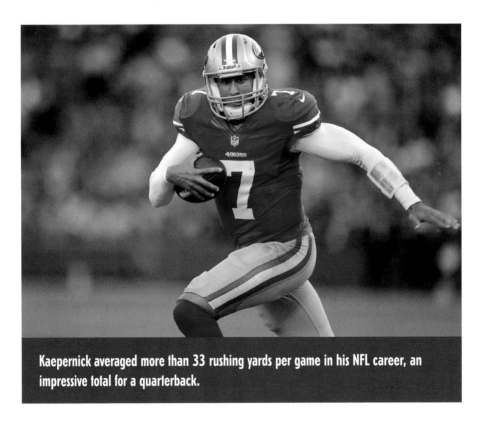

Kaepernick averaged more than 33 rushing yards per game in his NFL career, an impressive total for a quarterback.

with Kaepernick. He
finished the season strong,
including a huge win
against Tom Brady and the
Patriots in New England.

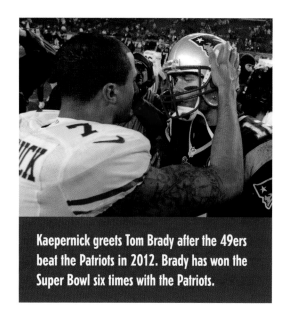

Kaepernick greets Tom Brady after the 49ers beat the Patriots in 2012. Brady has won the Super Bowl six times with the Patriots.

After the Patriots
game, more people's
eyes opened to what
Kaepernick could do. TV
analyst Cris Collinsworth
was among them. He said,
"[Kaepernick] may have
played the best game at quarterback, certainly one of the
best games, that I've ever seen."

The 49ers cruised into the playoffs. Kaepernick's first
NFL playoff game was against the powerhouse Packers,
led by the league's reigning Most Valuable Player, Aaron
Rodgers. If Kaepernick felt pressure, he didn't show it. He
passed for 263 yards and two touchdowns, and he ran for
181 yards. That set an NFL single-game record for most
rushing yards by a quarterback. He also picked up two
rushing touchdowns. San Francisco won 45–31.

Kaepernick and the 49ers defeated the Atlanta Falcons
in the conference championship and advanced to the 2013
Super Bowl. Facing off against the Baltimore Ravens, the
game could not have started worse for San Francisco.
The 49ers fell behind by 22 points in the third quarter.
That's when things got weird. Suddenly, the lights and
scoreboards in the Louisiana Superdome went out.

Kaepernick rushed for 62 yards against the Ravens, the second-highest total ever for a quarterback in a Super Bowl.

Nobody knew what caused the power failure. But when the lights came back on 34 minutes later, the 49ers looked like a different team. Kaepernick tossed a long touchdown pass. San Francisco scored two more times before Kaepernick ran in a 15-yard touchdown. In the end, the furious comeback fell just short. Baltimore held on for a 34–31 victory.

In spite of the heartbreaking loss in the bizarre blackout game, the future looked bright for Kaepernick. He had shown the world how special he could be as a player. Before the start of the next season, ESPN analyst Ron Jaworski said, "I truly believe Colin Kaepernick could be one of the greatest quarterbacks ever. I love his skill set. I think the sky's the limit."

Kaepernick was the number one quarterback in San Francisco to start the 2013 season, and he had a great year. He led the team to a 12–4 record and another trip to the playoffs. But in the conference title game, San Francisco lost to the Seattle Seahawks. Seattle would go on to win the Super Bowl.

That off-season, Kaepernick signed a six-year contract extension with the 49ers worth $126 million. He was making a lot of money from product endorsements as well, a benefit of being a high-profile athlete. But his performance in 2014 was not as sharp as it had been. The team went 8–8 and missed the playoffs. In 2015 Kaepernick struggled again. During a particularly bad performance in Week 8 against the Rams, the 49ers benched him for backup quarterback Blaine Gabbert. Kaepernick had surgery on his left shoulder, which he had injured several weeks earlier. He would miss the rest of the season.

Kaepernick was ready to play again in 2016. But for the first time in two years, he didn't know what his role would be. He'd have to compete with Gabbert for the job of starting quarterback.

Playing time wasn't the only thing on Kaepernick's mind. With police violence against minorities in the news and racially charged anger growing on social

Running quarterbacks take a lot of hits, and Kaepernick hurt his shoulder when he was tackled during a game against Green Bay.

media, he began to think about his role in society. He wanted to make a difference. He wanted to use his position as a star athlete to raise awareness of these problems and create change. But how?

A Powerful Voice

As a star in the NFL, Kaepernick received intense attention from fans and media, much of it negative and racist. One sports columnist criticized him for having tattoos, saying he looked as if he "just got paroled" from jail. Kaepernick had been learning more about African American history and culture since childhood. But because of the increasing attention, he began yearning to learn even more. Over the summer of 2016, he attended a class at the University of California, Berkeley, on how black people are represented in US culture.

Kaepernick's social media accounts show that he was changing. Early in his career, he had mainly posted football-related items. But in 2016, he began posting about race and social justice. That summer the killing of two more black men by police captured Kaepernick's attention. He wrote online that people of color were being attacked. Protesters demonstrated against police violence in Louisiana and Minnesota, where the men had been killed.

Protest movements against police violence had been growing in recent years. Activists Alicia Garza, Patrisse

People protest in Baton Rouge, Louisiana, in 2016 after 37-year-old black man Alton Sterling was killed by police.

Cullors, and Opal Tometi started Black Lives Matter in 2013 in response to the killing of black teen Trayvon Martin in Florida by neighborhood-watch volunteer George Zimmerman. The movement gained attention after another unarmed black teenage boy was shot and killed by police in Ferguson, Missouri, in the summer of 2014. What started as a hashtag, #blacklivesmatter, grew into a global organization with the mission of ending violence inflicted on black communities. Kaepernick wanted to join this mission. In August 2016, when the football preseason began, he was ready to take a stand—by sitting.

Kaepernick knew that his protest would not go over well with a lot of people. That included some of his teammates, coaches, and the team owner. But he didn't seek anyone's permission to take action.

Fighting for Civil Rights

People of color have long fought for equal rights and better treatment in the United States. Kaepernick's protest was part of a larger movement that activists have engaged in for generations. During the US civil rights movement in the 1950s and 1960s, black Americans and their allies fought for and gained many rights. During this time, segregation in the US military, in schools, and on public transportation became illegal. The Civil Rights Act of 1964 outlawed employment discrimination, and the Voting Rights Act of 1965 helped protect the right to vote for all citizens.

Athletes have used their platforms to take a stand on important issues before, and some paid a steep price. In 1996 National Basketball Association player Mahmoud Abdul-Rauf refused to acknowledge the flag and anthem at games. The reasons he gave were similar to Kaepernick's, and the league suspended Abdul-Rauf. He returned after two days when he  agreed to stand for the anthem. Outspoken athletes, especially black athletes, receive huge amounts of criticism and hatred online and in sports media. Fans in the stands even verbally attack them.

This gathering in protest of Philando Castile's death took place in Minneapolis, Minnesota, in 2016.

"This is not something that I am going to run by anybody," he said to NFL Media. "I am not looking for approval. I have to stand up for people that are oppressed." What he said next made it clear that he knew what was at stake. "If they take football away, my endorsements from me, I know that I stood up for what is right."

Not all NFL players were on Kaepernick's side. Some disagreed with his politics. Others felt he was disrespecting the United States. Some agreed with his message, but not his method of protest. One man, Nate Boyer, was a former US Army soldier who had a very short career as a punter with the Seattle Seahawks. He wrote an open letter to Kaepernick that was published on the *Army Times* website.

Boyer started his letter by saying he was a fan of Kaepernick's football career. He said he knew Kaepernick supported the military because the quarterback had signed a football for Boyer's charity and written "God bless our troops!" on it. Boyer said he knew that racism was still a big problem. And he admitted that because he was a white person in the United States, he could

Some fans began a counterprotest of Kaepernick's message by bringing signs to games.

not know what racism felt like. He could never know what it was like to walk in Kaepernick's shoes.

Then Boyer explained how much the US flag meant to him. He had always felt a lot of pride in it. In the army, he had fought alongside soldiers who had died defending the flag and what it stood for. Boyer talked about the one NFL game he played in and how proud he felt to stand for the national anthem. He said his feelings would have been hurt if he had seen a teammate sitting on the bench. Boyer did not judge Kaepernick for his protest. He admitted that he was angry when he first heard about it. But Boyer wanted to understand Kaepernick and his message.

The letter touched Kaepernick. He wanted to learn more about Boyer's viewpoint, so he contacted the former punter. The two met in a hotel lobby and talked. Boyer said he wished that Kaepernick would stand for the anthem, but Kaepernick was determined to continue his protest. Then Boyer suggested that he kneel instead of sit. He felt this would be more respectful to the flag but still bring attention to police violence and racial injustice.

Kaepernick agreed. He did not want his protest to be disrespectful to the US military. He had been clear about that from the beginning. He told the press he had "great respect for the men and women that have fought for this country."

When the anthem played at the next 49ers preseason game, Kaepernick kneeled. His teammate, Eric Reid, joined him. At a game later that night, a Seattle player sat for the anthem. Days later, soccer player Megan Rapinoe of the US national team knelt before a game against the Netherlands. The next week, Denver Broncos linebacker Brandon Marshall became the first player to kneel before an NFL regular season game.

Kaepernick and Eric Reid kneel during the national anthem on September 1, 2016. Nate Boyer stands to Kaepernick's left.

By now, just about everyone was paying attention to the growing protest. Reporters, analysts, players, fans— even politicians and people who didn't care about football were talking about the protest and what it meant. In spite of Kaepernick's intentions and his decision to kneel instead of sit, many said the protest was anti-military. Some said a millionaire athlete with a comfortable life didn't know about oppression. They said if he didn't like his country, he should leave. Still others said he should find a different way to protest that wasn't so controversial.

The controversy was the point. If he had chosen a

Brandon Marshall kneels before a regular season game. Marshall and Kaepernick were roommates in college.

different way to protest, far fewer people would have noticed and the discussion would have ended quickly. Kaepernick's decision to kneel during the national anthem ensured that everyone was talking about police violence and social justice. And for that, many saw him as a hero.

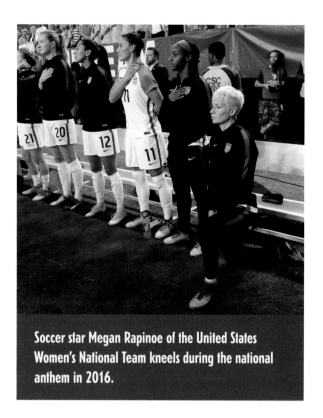

Soccer star Megan Rapinoe of the United States Women's National Team kneels during the national anthem in 2016.

The Protest and the Noise

As the 2016 regular season wore on, Kaepernick kept kneeling for "The Star Spangled Banner." Many players across the league and in other sports joined him. He won back the starting quarterback job partway through the season, but he couldn't save the 49ers from a losing record. They went 2–14, and Kaepernick's performance was average.

His activism wasn't limited to kneeling before games. In September he pledged to donate $1 million to charities working in oppressed communities. He would

Kaepernick works with Jessica's House, a group that provides grief support for young people in the Turlock area.

donate $100,000 every month for ten months to small organizations doing work in local communities. When he gave $25,000 to the I Will Not Die Young Campaign, an organization that helps at-risk youth in Milwaukee, founder Muhibb Dyer thought it was a prank at first. Dyer later talked about how important the money was. "Having [Kaepernick] reach out to us is like a lifeline to continue the work that we do," Dyer said.

Kaepernick also started holding free Know Your Rights Camp events for kids. The mission of the camps was to help kids stand up for themselves and seek a better future. One important aspect was teaching kids how to interact with police to stay safe. The instruction focused on ten rights that every child should know. The first was, "You have the right to be free." That sentence was repeated with a different word at the end each time: healthy, brilliant, safe, loved, courageous, alive, trusted, and educated. The last sentence was, "You have the right to know your rights."

Kids in camp learned about financial literacy and living a healthy lifestyle. They learned about applying to college. Kaepernick also wanted the kids to think about their heritage. He had taken a DNA test and learned that some of his ancestors came from Ghana and Nigeria. He said, "It changed everything for me. It helped me know that my history did not begin with being adopted. It did not begin with slavery." Kaepernick gave campers DNA kits to trace their heritage. They could learn more

During a game in 2017, Eric Reid wore cleats that said "Know Your Rights Camp" in honor of Kaepernick's work.

about who they were and where they came from.

Kaepernick ran the camps himself with the help of close friends. He didn't have corporate sponsors. He didn't invite the media. He wanted the camps to be just for the kids.

Meanwhile, the public's intensity of feelings about Kaepernick increased. Many in the conservative media trashed him. Writers insulted him and questioned his motives. Others said his protests were meaningless empty gestures. If he really wanted to make change, they said, he should donate money. They had no idea about Kaepernick's charity work and donations.

Many people felt that it was Kaepernick's duty as a citizen of the United States to show respect for the country's flag and anthem.

Kaepernick had supporters and detractors at every game.

Kaepernick's work was anything but meaningless. Besides his donations and efforts to promote social justice, his passion had inspired others. The 49ers donated $1 million to improve racial and economic inequality in the San Francisco area. Players across the NFL were joining him in kneeling. According to one report, more than 70 players talked in a group chat about "what Kaep started."

Players weren't the only ones talking and thinking about what it means to stand for the national anthem. All around the country, even around the world, people were examining their feelings. Why do we stand for the anthem? What do I know about racism and police violence? Can you be patriotic and still criticize your country? What Kaep had started was a movement.

Kaepernick's movement was especially popular with young people. This group rallied in New York in 2017 to support his message.

At the end of the season, Kaepernick's teammates voted him the winner of the Len Eshmont Award for inspiring play, the team's highest honor. But that winter, Kaepernick found out that the 49ers were going to release him to avoid paying the millions of dollars left on his contract. He chose to become a free agent instead.

Kaepernick didn't know it then, but he had almost certainly played his last game as an NFL quarterback. No team signed him. Some team officials said his protests would be a distraction. Others said that the Super Bowl quarterback wasn't good enough. Many of the teams' wealthy white owners privately said they hated Kaepernick. They simply didn't want him to have a job.

That summer another story of racial tension made news. A group of white nationalists held a rally in Charlottesville, Virginia. Counterprotesters gathered to reject white supremacy. The two groups clashed violently. A white nationalist drove his car into a group of counterprotesters and killed a woman.

The country was emotional, angry—and divided. In the middle of it all, Kaepernick had become a symbol. People chose sides in the massive cultural debate. For some, there was no middle ground.

White nationalists in Charlottesville carried Confederate flags, a symbol of racism to many people.

A Polarizing Figure

Kaepernick remained out of football for all of 2017. He was young and healthy. He'd had much more NFL success than other free agent quarterbacks, yet teams refused to sign him. Kaepernick filed a lawsuit against the NFL. It accused the owners of colluding—or secretly and unlawfully cooperating—to keep him out of a job. His attorney said athletes who protest peacefully should be free of punishment. Kaepernick ended his lawsuit in February 2019 when the NFL agreed to pay him an undisclosed amount of money.

And yet, even though he was absent from football, the protest he inspired continued to grow. More players than ever were kneeling during the national anthem, including some white players. The movement's success angered Trump. He used a speech to cast those who kneeled as villains. He even used a curse word to describe them.

Donald Trump made it clear that he wouldn't tolerate player protests if he ran the NFL.

Members of the Minnesota Lynx basketball team stand arm in arm during the national anthem.

Days later, players from every NFL team had a defiant response to the president's words: they protested. Some knelt during the national anthem. Others thrust a fist into the sky. Even some coaches and team owners joined the players on the field, locking arms in unity.

Athletes in other sports protested too. In the Women's National Basketball Association championship series, the Los Angeles Sparks walked out as a team during the anthem. Their opponents, the Minnesota Lynx, linked arms while standing. High school athletes around the United States knelt before games as well.

Many fans, however, identified with Trump's anger. They saw the protests as rude. To them, the protests were disrespectful to the military and law enforcement, and the protesters were ungrateful for the benefits of living in the United States. As these people registered their disgust on social media, team owners began to worry. To try to avoid losing fans and money, they made a rule that required players to stand for the anthem.

The NFL Players Association, a union that represents all NFL players, filed a grievance in response. It said the rule violated their right to free speech. Philadelphia Eagles player Malcolm Jenkins said, "Everyone loses when voices get stifled." League officials suspended the rule, and owners and players continue to discuss a solution that works for both sides.

In May 2018 NFL commissioner Roger Goodell announced that all players on the field must stand for the national anthem. The league suspended the rule less than two months later.

More Activist Athletes

The year 2018 marked the 50th anniversary of Tommie Smith and John Carlos's protest at the 1968 Olympic Games in Mexico City, Mexico. The two track stars stood on the podium wearing their Olympic medals while "The Star Spangled Banner" played, their fists raised. It was a symbol of protest against civil rights abuses in America. Another activist athlete, boxer Muhammad Ali, refused to serve in the Vietnam War (1957–1975) and spoke out against the fighting there. Many people publicly demonized Smith, Carlos, and Ali for their actions. Carlos and Smith received death threats, and Ali served time in jail for refusing to fight in the war. Like Kaepernick, Ali couldn't compete during some of the prime years of his career. These athletes and many others have used their platforms to stand up for issues that were important to them.

As the NFL played games in 2017 without him, Kaepernick's supporters criticized owners for not signing him, and many athletes continued to protest. As for Kaepernick, he wasn't just waiting around for a job opportunity. To understand his African roots, he took a trip to Ghana. He spent time with historians and scholars as well as activists and artists to learn more about his heritage.

Kaepernick wasn't welcome in the NFL in 2018, giving him plenty of time to focus on social activism and learning more about his heritage.

As the 2018 NFL season was about to get underway, he still didn't have a team. But before the first game, the sports gear company Nike released a new ad featuring Kaepernick. It showed a close-up photo of his face with the lines, "Believe in something. Even if it means sacrificing everything."

The message was clear. Nike was standing behind Kaepernick and his protest. The ad reignited the public controversy. Many people were angry that Nike would take his side in such a high-profile way. In response, some posted videos and photos of themselves on social media burning Nike clothes. Others loved the ad. Supporters such as tennis superstar Serena Williams publicly applauded the move. Kaepernick remained silent. Without uttering a word, he had focused the public's attention on the topics of civil rights and police brutality once again. Just as he had wanted.

Charity and community service also took up much of his time in 2017 and 2018. He kept holding Know Your Rights Camps. He raised money for hunger relief in Somalia and helped convince Turkish Airlines to fly 60 tons (54 t) of food there. He also fulfilled his promise to donate $1 million to charities.

Many organizations recognized his impact on society. The magazine *GQ* named him its Citizen of the Year. *Sports Illustrated* gave him the Muhammad Ali Legacy Award, which honors an athlete's positive

Nike's worldwide advertising campaign with Kaepernick included TV ads, billboards, and more.

influence on the world. The American Civil Liberties Union granted him the Eason Monroe Courageous Advocate Award for his work bringing attention to oppression in America.

In 2018 Kaepernick was recognized by the global human rights organization Amnesty International. It gave him the Ambassador of Conscience Award, its highest honor. "We rely on people like Colin, when they feel like they simply cannot be silenced, to speak out and inspire huge numbers of people, despite the professional and personal risks," said Augusta Quiney of Amnesty International.

Because of Kaepernick's protest, he may never play pro football again. He lost his career, but he gained a powerful voice. His actions, which started as a one-man silent protest, sparked a worldwide discussion

Kaepernick speaks while being honored by the American Civil Liberties Union of Southern California in 2017.

Fans take a selfie with Kaepernick in April 2018 after he won the Ambassador of Conscience Award.

and joined a larger movement for social justice. He has raised awareness about oppression and police violence and inspired people to take action for peace and equality.

That's more than a gesture. It's more than a movement. It is real change.

IMPORTANT DATES

1987   Colin Kaepernick is born on November 3 and adopted by Rick and Teresa Kaepernick at five weeks old.

1991   He moves with his family to Turlock, California.

2006   He graduates from Pitman High School.

2007   He joins the University of Nevada football team.

2010   He leads Nevada to a 34–31 overtime victory against the previously undefeated Boise State Broncos on November 26. He becomes the only collegiate quarterback to throw for more than 10,000 yards and rush for more than 4,000 in a career.

2011   He is drafted by the San Francisco 49ers on April 29.

2012   He replaces Alex Smith as San Francisco's starting quarterback.

2013   He nearly leads a dramatic comeback win in the Super Bowl, but San Francisco loses to Baltimore, on February 3.

2014   He signs a six-year contract extension with the 49ers on June 4.

2015 After erratic play, he is benched on November 8.

2016 He sits during the national anthem before preseason games on August 14, 20, and 26. He takes a knee during the anthem on September 1 and kneels for the anthem before every regular-season game.

He holds the first Know Your Rights Camp events.

2017 He leaves the 49ers and goes unsigned for the entire season.

2018 He appears in ads for Nike that reignite discussions of his protest.

Amnesty International gives him the Ambassador of Conscience Award.

2019 He settles his collusion lawsuit with the NFL.

SOURCE NOTES

10 Steve Wyche, "Colin Kaepernick Explains Why He Sat during National Anthem," NFL, August 27, 2016, http://www.nfl.com /news/story/0ap3000000691077/article/colin-kaepernick -explains-protest-of-national-anthem.

12 Martenzie Johnson, "Colin Kaepernick's Parents Break Silence: 'We Absolutely Do Support Him,'" *ESPN*, December 10, 2016, http://www.espn.com/nfl/story/_/id/18247113/colin-kaepernick -parents-break-silence-speak-support-criticized-quarterback.

15 John Branch, "The Awakening of Colin Kaepernick," *New York Times*, September 7, 2017, https://www.nytimes.com/2017/09/07 /sports/colin-kaepernick-nfl-protests.html.

17 Branch.

18 Branch.

20 Branch.

23 Wyche, "Colin Kaepernick."

23 Nate Boyer, "An Open Letter to Colin Kaepernick, from a Green Beret-Turned-Long Snapper," *Army Times*, August 30, 2016, https://www.armytimes.com/opinion/2016/08/30/an-open-letter -to-colin-kaepernick-from-a-green-beret-turned-long-snapper/.

23 Boyer.

25 Branch, "Awakening."

28 Branch.

29 Know Your Rights Camp, accessed March 24, 2019, https:// knowyourrightscamp.com/about/.

29 Shaun King, "Colin Kaepernick's 'I Know My Rights Camp' Cements His Status as a Cultural Superhero in the Black Community," *New York Daily News*, October 29, 2016, https://www.nydailynews.com/news/national/king-kaepernick-camp-cements-status-black-community-article-1.2850326.

31 Josh Levin, "Colin Kaepernick's Protest Is Working," Slate, September 12, 2016, https://slate.com/culture/2016/09/colin-kaepernicks-protest-is-working.html.

36 Adam Stites, "What the NFL's Halted Anthem Policy Means for the Players, Teams, and League," SB Nation, September 9, 2018, https://www.sbnation.com/2018/7/23/17596078/nfl-national-anthem-policy-ramifications.

38 Will Burns, "With New Kaepernick Ad, What Does Nike Believe In?" *Forbes*, September 4, 2018, https://www.forbes.com/sites/willburns/2018/09/04/with-new-kaepernick-ad-what-does-nike-believe-in/#5d4653371081.

40 Sean Gregory, "Colin Kaepernick Wins Amnesty International's Highest Honor," *Time*, April 21, 2018, http://time.com/5248606/colin-kaepernick-wins-amnesty-internationals-ambassador-of-conscience-award/.

SELECTED BIBLIOGRAPHY

Adelson, Andrea. "Colin Kaepernick More Than Star QB." *ESPN*, October 4, 2010. http://www.espn.com/college-football/news/story?id=5644658.

Branch, John. "The Awakening of Colin Kaepernick." *New York Times*, September 7, 2017. https://www.nytimes.com/2017/09/07/sports/colin-kaepernick-nfl-protests.html.

Hoffman, Benjamin, and Talya Minsberg. "The Deafening Silence of Colin Kaepernick." *New York Times*, September 4, 2018. https://www.nytimes.com/2018/09/04/sports/colin-kaepernick-nfl-anthem-kneeling.html.

Levin, Josh. "Colin Kaepernick Won." Slate, August 18, 2017. https://slate.com/sports/2017/08/colin-kaepernicks-protest-cost-him-his-job-but-started-a-movement.html.

Meyersohn, Nathaniel. "Nike Takes Sides, Tapping Colin Kaepernick for New 'Just Do It' Ad." *CNN*, September 4, 2018. https://money.cnn.com/2018/09/03/news/companies/colin-kaepernick-nike-just-do-it/index.html.

Wyche, Steve. "Colin Kaepernick Explains Why He Sat during National Anthem." NFL, August 27, 2016. http://www.nfl.com/news/story/0ap3000000691077/article/colin-kaepernick-explains-protest-of-national-anthem.

FURTHER READING

BOOKS

Braun, Eric. *The Civil Rights Movement.* Minneapolis: Lerner Publications, 2019. Learn more about the history of the civil rights movement.

Doeden, Matt. *More Than a Game: Race, Gender, and Politics in Sports.* Minneapolis: Millbrook Press, 2020. Find out more about the history of sports and social movements.

Harris, Duchess. *Black Lives Matter.* Minneapolis: Core Library, 2018. Read about the movement working to stop violence inflicted on communities of color.

WEBSITES

Amnesty International
https://www.amnesty.org/en
Amnesty International's website has news about human rights from around the world.

Black Lives Matter
https://blacklivesmatter.com
Learn about upcoming events, access resources for promoting social justice, and much more.

Know Your Rights Camp
https://knowyourrightscamp.com
Find information about Know Your Rights Camp events.

INDEX